50 Delicious Comfort Sandwich Recipes for Home

By: Kelly Johnson

Table of Contents

- Classic Grilled Cheese
- BLT
- Turkey Club
- Reuben
- Philly Cheesesteak
- Cuban Sandwich
- Pastrami on Rye
- Chicken Parmesan Sandwich
- French Dip
- Sloppy Joes
- Egg Salad Sandwich
- Tuna Melt
- Roast Beef and Cheddar
- Caprese Sandwich
- Pulled Pork Sandwich
- Ham and Swiss
- Grilled Chicken Caesar Wrap
- Buffalo Chicken Sandwich
- Meatball Sub
- Veggie and Hummus Wrap
- Monte Cristo
- Avocado Toast Sandwich
- BBQ Chicken Sandwich
- Italian Sausage Sandwich
- Turkey and Cranberry Sandwich
- Chicken Salad Sandwich
- Eggplant Parmesan Sandwich
- PBLT (Pancetta, Bacon, Lettuce, Tomato)
- Mushroom and Swiss Burger
- Cheeseburger
- Pita Pocket with Falafel
- Lamb Gyro

- Thai Peanut Chicken Sandwich
- Breakfast Burrito Wrap
- Lobster Roll
- Corned Beef on Rye
- Falafel Sandwich
- Grilled Veggie Sandwich
- Hot Ham and Cheese
- Spicy Italian Sub
- Chicken and Waffles Sandwich
- Crispy Fish Sandwich
- Tandoori Chicken Sandwich
- Pulled Beef Brisket Sandwich
- Pork Schnitzel Sandwich
- Pork Belly Banh Mi
- Roasted Red Pepper and Goat Cheese Sandwich
- Cheddar and Apple Sandwich
- Black Bean and Avocado Wrap
- Buffalo Cauliflower Sandwich

Classic Grilled Cheese

For a classic grilled cheese, you'll need:

- 2 slices of bread (white or whole wheat)
- 2 tablespoons of butter
- 2 slices of cheddar cheese (or your choice)

Instructions:

1. Butter one side of each bread slice.
2. Place one slice, butter-side down, in a skillet over medium heat.
3. Add the cheese slices on top.
4. Place the second slice of bread on top, butter-side up.
5. Cook until golden brown, then flip and cook the other side until the cheese is melted.

Enjoy your ultimate comfort food!

BLT

Ingredients:

- 2 slices of bread (white, whole wheat, or your favorite type)
- 2-3 slices of bacon
- 2-3 leaves of lettuce (such as romaine or iceberg)
- 1 tomato, sliced
- Mayonnaise
- Salt and pepper (to taste)

Instructions:

1. **Cook the Bacon:**
    - In a skillet over medium heat, cook the bacon slices until crispy. This usually takes about 4-6 minutes per side.
    - Remove the bacon and place it on a paper towel-lined plate to drain excess grease.
2. **Toast the Bread:**
    - Toast the bread slices in a toaster or in a skillet until they are golden brown.
3. **Assemble the Sandwich:**
    - Spread mayonnaise on one side of each slice of toast.
    - On one slice of toast, layer the lettuce, tomato slices, and bacon.
    - Season the tomato slices with a pinch of salt and pepper if desired.
    - Top with the second slice of toast, mayonnaise side down.
4. **Serve:**
    - Cut the sandwich in half, if you like, and enjoy!

Feel free to customize with additional toppings or variations like avocado or a different type of bacon.

Turkey Club

Ingredients:

- 3 slices of bread (white, whole wheat, or toasted)
- 2-3 slices of turkey breast (deli-style or roasted)
- 2-3 slices of bacon, cooked until crispy
- 2 leaves of lettuce
- 2 slices of tomato
- Mayonnaise
- Salt and pepper (to taste)

Instructions:

1. **Prepare the Bread:**
   - Toast the bread slices if desired.
2. **Assemble the Sandwich:**
   - Spread mayonnaise on one side of each slice of bread.
   - On one slice, layer the lettuce, turkey slices, and bacon.
   - Add the tomato slices, and season with salt and pepper.
   - Top with another slice of bread, mayonnaise side down.
   - Add more turkey, bacon, and another layer of lettuce and tomato.
   - Finish with the final slice of bread, mayonnaise side down.
3. **Serve:**
   - Cut the sandwich into quarters and secure with toothpicks if needed.

Enjoy this hearty and satisfying sandwich!

Reuben

Ingredients:

- 2 slices of rye bread
- 2-3 ounces of corned beef (sliced)
- 1 slice of Swiss cheese
- 2 tablespoons of sauerkraut (drained)
- 2 tablespoons of Russian or Thousand Island dressing
- 1-2 tablespoons of butter

Instructions:

1. **Prepare the Bread:**
   - Butter one side of each bread slice.
2. **Assemble the Sandwich:**
   - On the non-buttered side of one slice, spread the dressing.
   - Layer the corned beef, Swiss cheese, and sauerkraut.
   - Spread dressing on the non-buttered side of the second slice of bread, then place it on top of the filling.
3. **Grill the Sandwich:**
   - Heat a skillet over medium heat.
   - Place the sandwich in the skillet and grill until golden brown and the cheese is melted, about 4-5 minutes per side.
4. **Serve:**
   - Slice and enjoy this flavorful classic!

Philly Cheesesteak

Ingredients:

- 1 lb thinly sliced beef (ribeye or sirloin)
- 1-2 tablespoons olive oil
- 1 onion, sliced
- 1 bell pepper, sliced (optional)
- 4 slices provolone or American cheese
- 2-4 hoagie rolls or sub rolls
- Salt and pepper (to taste)

Instructions:

1. **Cook the Beef:**
    - Heat olive oil in a skillet over medium-high heat.
    - Add the sliced beef, salt, and pepper. Cook until browned, about 2-3 minutes per side. Remove and set aside.
2. **Cook the Vegetables:**
    - In the same skillet, add the onions (and bell pepper if using). Cook until softened and slightly caramelized, about 5-7 minutes.
3. **Combine:**
    - Return the beef to the skillet with the onions and peppers. Mix well and cook for another minute.
4. **Assemble:**
    - Divide the beef mixture among the rolls. Top with cheese slices.
    - Place the sandwiches under a broiler or in a toaster oven for a few minutes until the cheese is melted.
5. **Serve:**
    - Enjoy your Philly Cheesesteak hot and gooey!

Cuban Sandwich

Ingredients:

- 1 loaf Cuban bread or French bread
- 4-6 ounces of roast pork, sliced
- 4-6 ounces of ham, sliced
- 2-3 slices of Swiss cheese
- 4-6 dill pickle slices
- Yellow mustard
- Butter (for grilling)

Instructions:

1. **Prepare the Bread:**
    - Slice the Cuban bread in half lengthwise.
2. **Assemble the Sandwich:**
    - Spread mustard on the inside of both bread halves.
    - Layer the roast pork, ham, cheese, and pickles on the bottom half.
3. **Grill the Sandwich:**
    - Close the sandwich with the top half of the bread.
    - Butter the outside of the bread. Place the sandwich in a hot skillet or a panini press.
    - Grill until the bread is crispy and golden, and the cheese is melted, about 4-5 minutes per side if using a skillet.
4. **Serve:**
    - Slice and enjoy the savory and tangy Cuban delight!

Pastrami on Rye

Ingredients:

- 2 slices of rye bread
- 4-6 ounces of pastrami, sliced
- 2 tablespoons of mustard (yellow or deli-style)
- Pickles (optional)

Instructions:

1. **Prepare the Bread:**
   - Toast the rye bread if desired.
2. **Assemble the Sandwich:**
   - Spread mustard on one side of each slice of bread.
   - Layer the pastrami on one slice of bread.
3. **Finish:**
   - Top with the second slice of bread, mustard side down.
   - Add pickles on the side if you like.
4. **Serve:**
   - Slice the sandwich in half and enjoy this classic deli favorite!

Chicken Parmesan Sandwich

Ingredients:

- 1 chicken breast, breaded and cooked (or use chicken tenders)
- 1 cup marinara sauce
- 1 slice of mozzarella cheese
- 1 slice of Parmesan cheese (optional)
- 1 hoagie roll or sub roll
- 1-2 tablespoons olive oil
- Fresh basil or parsley (optional)

Instructions:

1. **Prepare the Chicken:**
   - Heat the marinara sauce in a pan.
   - If not already done, bread and cook the chicken breast until crispy and cooked through.
2. **Assemble the Sandwich:**
   - Slice the hoagie roll and drizzle the inside with olive oil.
   - Place the cooked chicken on the roll.
   - Spoon marinara sauce over the chicken.
   - Top with mozzarella and Parmesan cheese.
3. **Grill or Broil:**
   - If desired, broil in the oven or toast in a skillet until the cheese is melted and bubbly.
4. **Serve:**
   - Garnish with fresh basil or parsley if using. Slice and enjoy!

French Dip

Ingredients:

- 1 lb beef roast (such as ribeye or sirloin), thinly sliced
- 1 large French baguette or 4 hoagie rolls
- 1 large onion, sliced
- 2 cups beef broth
- 1 cup water
- 1 tablespoon soy sauce
- 1 tablespoon Worcestershire sauce
- 2-3 tablespoons olive oil
- Salt and pepper (to taste)
- Optional: provolone or Swiss cheese slices

Instructions:

1. **Prepare the Beef:**
   - Season the beef slices with salt and pepper.
   - Heat 1 tablespoon of olive oil in a skillet over medium-high heat.
   - Add the beef slices and cook until browned and cooked through, about 2-3 minutes per side. Remove and set aside.
2. **Cook the Onions:**
   - In the same skillet, add another tablespoon of olive oil.
   - Add the sliced onions and cook until caramelized, about 10-15 minutes, stirring occasionally.
3. **Prepare the Au Jus:**
   - In a saucepan, combine the beef broth, water, soy sauce, and Worcestershire sauce.
   - Bring to a simmer and cook for 5 minutes. Adjust seasoning with salt and pepper if needed.
4. **Assemble the Sandwich:**
   - Slice the baguette or hoagie rolls and lightly toast if desired.
   - Layer the beef slices on the bottom half of the bread.
   - Top with caramelized onions and cheese if using.
   - Place the top half of the bread on the sandwich.
5. **Serve:**
   - Serve the sandwiches with a cup of the warm au jus for dipping.

Enjoy your savory and satisfying French Dip!

Sloppy Joes

Ingredients:

- 1 lb ground beef
- 1 onion, finely chopped
- 1 bell pepper, finely chopped (optional)
- 2 cloves garlic, minced
- 1 cup ketchup
- 1/4 cup Worcestershire sauce
- 2 tablespoons brown sugar
- 1 tablespoon mustard
- Salt and pepper (to taste)
- 4 hamburger buns

Instructions:

1. **Cook the Beef:**
   - In a skillet over medium heat, cook the ground beef until browned, breaking it up with a spoon. Drain excess fat.
2. **Add Vegetables:**
   - Add the chopped onion, bell pepper (if using), and garlic. Cook until the vegetables are softened, about 5 minutes.
3. **Make the Sauce:**
   - Stir in ketchup, Worcestershire sauce, brown sugar, and mustard.
   - Simmer for 10-15 minutes, stirring occasionally, until the mixture is thickened. Season with salt and pepper.
4. **Assemble:**
   - Spoon the beef mixture onto the hamburger buns.
5. **Serve:**
   - Enjoy your messy, flavorful Sloppy Joes!

Egg Salad Sandwich

Ingredients:

- 6 large eggs
- 1/4 cup mayonnaise
- 1 tablespoon Dijon mustard
- 1 tablespoon chopped fresh chives or parsley (optional)
- Salt and pepper (to taste)
- 4 slices of bread (white, whole wheat, or your choice)
- Lettuce leaves (optional)
- Tomato slices (optional)

Instructions:

1. **Boil the Eggs:**
    - Place the eggs in a pot and cover with cold water. Bring to a boil over medium-high heat.
    - Once boiling, cover the pot, remove it from heat, and let it sit for 12 minutes.
    - Transfer the eggs to an ice bath to cool. Peel the eggs once cool enough to handle.
2. **Prepare the Egg Salad:**
    - Chop the boiled eggs into small pieces.
    - In a bowl, combine the chopped eggs with mayonnaise, Dijon mustard, and chives or parsley if using. Mix until well combined.
    - Season with salt and pepper to taste.
3. **Assemble the Sandwich:**
    - Spread the egg salad evenly onto two slices of bread.
    - If desired, add lettuce leaves and tomato slices before topping with the remaining bread slices.
4. **Serve:**
    - Cut the sandwich in half and enjoy!

This classic egg salad is creamy, flavorful, and perfect for a quick lunch.

Tuna Melt

Ingredients:

- 1 can (5 oz) tuna, drained
- 2 tablespoons mayonnaise
- 1 tablespoon Dijon mustard
- 1/4 cup finely chopped celery (optional)
- 1/4 cup finely chopped onion (optional)
- 1/4 cup shredded cheddar cheese or Swiss cheese
- 4 slices of bread (white, whole wheat, or your choice)
- 2 tablespoons butter
- Salt and pepper (to taste)
- Pickles or tomato slices (optional)

Instructions:

1. **Prepare the Tuna Salad:**
    - In a bowl, combine the drained tuna, mayonnaise, Dijon mustard, celery, and onion if using. Mix well.
    - Season with salt and pepper to taste.
2. **Assemble the Sandwich:**
    - Preheat a skillet over medium heat.
    - Spread butter on one side of each slice of bread.
    - On the non-buttered side of two slices, spread a generous amount of the tuna salad.
    - Top with shredded cheese.
    - Place the remaining slices of bread on top, buttered side up.
3. **Grill the Sandwich:**
    - Place the sandwiches in the skillet.
    - Cook until the bread is golden brown and crispy, and the cheese is melted, about 3-4 minutes per side. Press down slightly with a spatula to ensure even grilling.
4. **Serve:**
    - Slice the sandwiches in half if desired, and enjoy your warm, gooey Tuna Melt!

Feel free to add pickles or tomato slices for extra flavor if you like.

Roast Beef and Cheddar

Ingredients:

- 4 slices of rye or sourdough bread
- 6 ounces thinly sliced roast beef
- 2-3 slices of cheddar cheese
- 2 tablespoons horseradish sauce or Dijon mustard
- 1 tablespoon mayonnaise
- 1 tablespoon butter

Instructions:

1. **Prepare the Spread:**
   - In a small bowl, mix the horseradish sauce or Dijon mustard with mayonnaise.
2. **Assemble the Sandwich:**
   - Spread the sauce mixture on one side of each slice of bread.
   - Layer the roast beef evenly on two slices of bread.
   - Top with cheddar cheese slices.
3. **Grill the Sandwich:**
   - Close the sandwiches with the remaining bread slices.
   - Heat a skillet over medium heat and melt the butter in it.
   - Grill the sandwiches until the bread is golden brown and the cheese is melted, about 3-4 minutes per side.
4. **Serve:**
   - Cut in half and enjoy your savory Roast Beef and Cheddar sandwich!

Feel free to add extras like caramelized onions or pickles for extra flavor.

Caprese Sandwich

Ingredients:

- 1 ciabatta roll or baguette
- 1-2 ripe tomatoes, sliced
- 4-6 fresh mozzarella slices
- Fresh basil leaves
- 2 tablespoons balsamic glaze or reduction
- 2 tablespoons olive oil
- Salt and pepper (to taste)

Instructions:

1. **Prepare the Bread:**
   - Slice the ciabatta roll or baguette in half lengthwise.
2. **Assemble the Sandwich:**
   - Drizzle olive oil on the cut sides of the bread.
   - Layer tomato slices, mozzarella, and basil leaves on the bottom half of the bread.
   - Drizzle balsamic glaze over the top.
   - Season with salt and pepper to taste.
3. **Finish:**
   - Top with the other half of the bread.
4. **Serve:**
   - Enjoy the sandwich as is, or you can press it slightly for a more compact meal.

This Caprese Sandwich is light, flavorful, and perfect for a quick lunch or a summer picnic!

Pulled Pork Sandwich

Ingredients:

- 2-3 pounds pork shoulder (or pork butt)
- 1 cup BBQ sauce (your favorite)
- 1/2 cup apple cider vinegar
- 1/4 cup brown sugar
- 1 tablespoon smoked paprika
- 1 teaspoon garlic powder
- 1 teaspoon onion powder
- Salt and pepper (to taste)
- 4 hamburger buns
- Coleslaw (optional, for topping)

Instructions:

1. **Cook the Pork:**
    - Season the pork shoulder with smoked paprika, garlic powder, onion powder, salt, and pepper.
    - Place in a slow cooker. Combine BBQ sauce, apple cider vinegar, and brown sugar, then pour over the pork.
    - Cook on low for 8 hours or high for 4-5 hours, until the pork is tender and easy to shred.
2. **Shred the Pork:**
    - Remove the pork from the slow cooker and shred with two forks. Return the shredded pork to the slow cooker and mix with the sauce.
3. **Prepare the Buns:**
    - Toast the hamburger buns if desired.
4. **Assemble the Sandwich:**
    - Pile the pulled pork onto the bottom half of each bun.
    - Top with coleslaw if using, then place the top bun on.
5. **Serve:**
    - Enjoy your savory and satisfying Pulled Pork Sandwich!

Feel free to adjust the BBQ sauce to your taste for extra sweetness or tanginess.

Ham and Swiss

Ingredients:

- 2 slices of bread (white, whole wheat, rye, or your choice)
- 2-3 slices of ham (deli-style or cooked)
- 1-2 slices of Swiss cheese
- 1-2 tablespoons mustard (yellow or Dijon)
- 1-2 tablespoons mayonnaise (optional)
- Lettuce leaves or tomato slices (optional)
- Butter (for grilling, optional)

Instructions:

1. **Prepare the Bread:**
    - Spread mustard on one side of each slice of bread. Add mayonnaise if desired.
2. **Assemble the Sandwich:**
    - Place a slice of Swiss cheese on one slice of bread.
    - Layer the ham on top of the cheese.
    - Add another slice of Swiss cheese over the ham.
    - Top with the second slice of bread, mustard side down.
3. **Grill the Sandwich (Optional):**
    - Heat a skillet over medium heat.
    - Butter the outside of each slice of bread if you like a crispy, golden finish.
    - Place the sandwich in the skillet and grill until the bread is golden brown and the cheese is melted, about 3-4 minutes per side.
4. **Serve:**
    - If desired, add lettuce leaves or tomato slices before serving. Cut the sandwich in half and enjoy!

This Ham and Swiss Sandwich is quick to make and delicious either as a cold sandwich or a warm, grilled treat.

Grilled Chicken Caesar Wrap

Ingredients:

- 1 large flour tortilla or wrap
- 1 grilled chicken breast, sliced
- 2 cups romaine lettuce, chopped
- 1/4 cup Caesar dressing
- 1/4 cup grated Parmesan cheese
- 1/4 cup croutons (optional, for crunch)
- Salt and pepper (to taste)

Instructions:

1. **Prepare the Ingredients:**
    - Slice the grilled chicken breast into strips.
    - Chop the romaine lettuce.
2. **Assemble the Wrap:**
    - Spread Caesar dressing evenly over the tortilla.
    - Layer the chopped lettuce, sliced chicken, and Parmesan cheese on the tortilla.
    - Add croutons if using.
3. **Wrap and Serve:**
    - Season with salt and pepper if desired.
    - Roll up the tortilla tightly, folding in the sides as you go to enclose the filling.
4. **Cut and Enjoy:**
    - Slice the wrap in half and enjoy!

This wrap combines classic Caesar salad flavors with the convenience of a portable meal.

Buffalo Chicken Sandwich

Ingredients:

- 1 lb boneless, skinless chicken breasts or thighs
- 1 cup buffalo sauce (store-bought or homemade)
- 1/4 cup ranch or blue cheese dressing
- 4 hamburger buns
- Lettuce leaves (optional)
- Tomato slices (optional)
- Pickles (optional)
- 2 tablespoons olive oil
- Salt and pepper (to taste)
- 1 cup all-purpose flour
- 1 cup buttermilk (or regular milk with 1 tablespoon lemon juice)
- 1 teaspoon paprika
- 1/2 teaspoon garlic powder
- 1/2 teaspoon onion powder

Instructions:

1. **Prepare the Chicken:**
   - If using breasts, pound them to an even thickness for even cooking.
   - Season the chicken with salt and pepper.
2. **Coat the Chicken:**
   - Set up a breading station with three bowls: one with flour, one with buttermilk, and one with a mixture of flour, paprika, garlic powder, and onion powder.
   - Dip each piece of chicken in flour, then buttermilk, then the seasoned flour mixture.
3. **Cook the Chicken:**
   - Heat olive oil in a skillet over medium-high heat.
   - Fry the chicken until golden brown and cooked through, about 5-7 minutes per side. The internal temperature should reach 165°F (74°C).
   - Drain on paper towels.
4. **Prepare the Sandwiches:**
   - Toss the cooked chicken in buffalo sauce until well coated.
   - Toast the hamburger buns if desired.
5. **Assemble the Sandwich:**
   - Spread ranch or blue cheese dressing on the bottom half of each bun.
   - Place a piece of buffalo chicken on top.
   - Add lettuce, tomato slices, and pickles if using.
   - Top with the other half of the bun.
6. **Serve:**

- Slice the sandwiches in half if desired and enjoy!

This Buffalo Chicken Sandwich combines spicy buffalo sauce with cooling ranch or blue cheese for a deliciously balanced flavor.

Meatball Sub

Ingredients:

- 1 lb ground beef
- 1/4 cup bread crumbs
- 1/4 cup grated Parmesan cheese
- 1/4 cup chopped fresh parsley (or 1 tablespoon dried parsley)
- 1 egg
- 2 cloves garlic, minced
- 1 teaspoon dried oregano
- Salt and pepper (to taste)
- 1 cup marinara sauce (store-bought or homemade)
- 4 sub rolls or hoagie rolls
- 1-2 cups shredded mozzarella cheese
- Olive oil (for greasing)

Instructions:

1. **Prepare the Meatballs:**
   - Preheat your oven to 375°F (190°C).
   - In a large bowl, combine the ground beef, bread crumbs, Parmesan cheese, parsley, egg, minced garlic, oregano, salt, and pepper.
   - Mix until well combined, but don't overwork the meat.
   - Form the mixture into 12-15 meatballs, about 1.5 inches in diameter.
2. **Cook the Meatballs:**
   - Place the meatballs on a baking sheet lined with parchment paper or lightly greased.
   - Bake in the preheated oven for about 20-25 minutes, or until cooked through and browned. The internal temperature should be 160°F (71°C).
3. **Prepare the Sandwiches:**
   - Heat the marinara sauce in a saucepan over medium heat.
   - Once the meatballs are done, add them to the sauce and simmer for a few minutes to ensure they are well-coated and heated through.
4. **Assemble the Subs:**
   - Preheat your broiler or oven to 400°F (200°C) if you want to toast the rolls.
   - Slice the sub rolls and lightly toast them if desired.
   - Place a few meatballs in each roll, then spoon extra marinara sauce over the top.
   - Sprinkle shredded mozzarella cheese over the meatballs.
5. **Broil the Subs:**
   - Place the assembled subs under the broiler for 2-4 minutes, or until the cheese is melted and bubbly. Watch carefully to avoid burning.
6. **Serve:**

- Enjoy your delicious Meatball Subs hot!

Feel free to add extra toppings like sliced jalapeños or a sprinkle of Italian seasoning for added flavor.

Veggie and Hummus Wrap

Ingredients:

- 1 large flour tortilla or wrap
- 1/2 cup hummus (store-bought or homemade)
- 1/2 cup shredded carrots
- 1/2 cup cucumber, sliced into thin strips
- 1/2 cup bell pepper, sliced into thin strips (any color)
- 1/2 avocado, sliced
- 1 cup baby spinach or mixed greens
- 1/4 cup cherry tomatoes, halved
- Salt and pepper (to taste)
- Optional: Feta cheese, olives, or sprouts for extra flavor

Instructions:

1. **Prepare the Ingredients:**
   - Wash and slice the vegetables as needed.
   - If using, crumble the feta cheese and prepare any other optional toppings.
2. **Assemble the Wrap:**
   - Spread the hummus evenly over the tortilla, leaving about an inch border around the edges.
   - Layer the shredded carrots, cucumber strips, bell pepper strips, avocado slices, spinach, and cherry tomatoes on top of the hummus.
   - Season with a pinch of salt and pepper. Add any optional toppings like feta cheese or sprouts.
3. **Wrap It Up:**
   - Fold in the sides of the tortilla and then roll it up tightly from the bottom to enclose the filling.
4. **Serve:**
   - Slice the wrap in half if desired and enjoy!

This Veggie and Hummus Wrap is fresh, nutritious, and perfect for a quick lunch or light dinner.

Monte Cristo

Ingredients:

- 4 slices of bread (white or whole wheat)
- 2-3 slices of ham
- 2-3 slices of turkey (or chicken)
- 2 slices of Swiss cheese
- 2 eggs
- 1/2 cup milk
- 1 tablespoon Dijon mustard
- 1 tablespoon mayonnaise
- 1 tablespoon butter
- Powdered sugar (for garnish, optional)
- Raspberry or strawberry jam (for dipping, optional)

Instructions:

1. **Prepare the Sandwich:**
    - Spread mayonnaise and Dijon mustard on one side of each slice of bread.
    - Layer ham, turkey, and Swiss cheese on two slices of bread.
    - Top with the remaining bread slices, mayonnaise and mustard sides facing the filling, to form two sandwiches.
2. **Prepare the Batter:**
    - In a shallow dish, whisk together the eggs and milk.
3. **Cook the Sandwiches:**
    - Heat a skillet over medium heat and melt 1 tablespoon of butter.
    - Dip each sandwich into the egg mixture, ensuring both sides are coated.
    - Place the sandwiches in the skillet and cook until golden brown on each side and the cheese is melted, about 3-4 minutes per side.
4. **Serve:**
    - Dust with powdered sugar if desired for a sweet touch.
    - Serve with raspberry or strawberry jam on the side for dipping.

This Monte Cristo Sandwich is a delightful combination of savory and sweet flavors, making it a delicious treat for breakfast, lunch, or dinner!

Avocado Toast Sandwich

Ingredients:

- 1 ripe avocado
- 2 slices of bread (whole grain, sourdough, or your choice)
- 1 tablespoon lemon juice
- Salt and pepper (to taste)
- Optional toppings: cherry tomatoes, radishes, arugula, or sprouts
- Optional add-ins: sliced turkey, cheese, or a fried egg

Instructions:

1. **Prepare the Avocado:**
    - Cut the avocado in half, remove the pit, and scoop the flesh into a bowl.
    - Mash the avocado with a fork until smooth but still slightly chunky.
    - Stir in lemon juice, and season with salt and pepper to taste.
2. **Toast the Bread:**
    - Toast the slices of bread until golden brown and crispy.
3. **Assemble the Sandwich:**
    - Spread the mashed avocado evenly over one side of each slice of toasted bread.
    - Add any optional toppings or add-ins you like, such as cherry tomatoes, radishes, arugula, or sprouts. If adding sliced turkey, cheese, or a fried egg, layer them on top of the avocado.
4. **Finish and Serve:**
    - Place the second slice of bread on top to complete the sandwich.
    - Slice the sandwich in half and enjoy!

This Avocado Toast Sandwich is versatile and can be customized with your favorite toppings and add-ins for a quick, healthy, and satisfying meal.

BBQ Chicken Sandwich

Ingredients:

- 2 cups cooked chicken (shredded or diced)
- 1 cup BBQ sauce (your favorite)
- 4 hamburger buns or sandwich rolls
- 1/4 cup coleslaw (optional, for topping)
- 1 tablespoon olive oil
- Salt and pepper (to taste)
- Pickles (optional)

Instructions:

1. **Prepare the Chicken:**
    - In a bowl, mix the cooked chicken with BBQ sauce until well coated.
2. **Heat the Chicken:**
    - Heat olive oil in a skillet over medium heat.
    - Add the BBQ chicken and cook until heated through, about 5 minutes. Season with salt and pepper if needed.
3. **Toast the Buns:**
    - Split and lightly toast the hamburger buns in a separate skillet or under a broiler until golden brown.
4. **Assemble the Sandwich:**
    - Pile the BBQ chicken onto the bottom half of each bun.
    - Top with coleslaw if using, and add pickles if desired.
    - Place the top half of the bun on top.
5. **Serve:**
    - Slice the sandwiches in half if desired and enjoy!

This BBQ Chicken Sandwich is flavorful and perfect for a quick lunch or casual dinner.

Italian Sausage Sandwich

Ingredients:

- 4 Italian sausages (pork or turkey)
- 4 hoagie rolls or sub rolls
- 1 cup marinara sauce
- 1 onion, sliced
- 1 bell pepper, sliced
- 2 tablespoons olive oil
- 1/2 cup shredded provolone or mozzarella cheese (optional)
- Salt and pepper (to taste)

Instructions:

1. **Cook the Sausages:**
   - Preheat your grill or skillet over medium heat.
   - Cook the sausages until browned and cooked through, about 8-10 minutes, turning occasionally.
2. **Sauté the Vegetables:**
   - Heat olive oil in a skillet over medium heat.
   - Add the sliced onion and bell pepper. Sauté until softened and caramelized, about 8 minutes. Season with salt and pepper.
3. **Heat the Sauce:**
   - In a small saucepan, warm the marinara sauce over low heat.
4. **Assemble the Sandwiches:**
   - Split and lightly toast the hoagie rolls if desired.
   - Place each cooked sausage in a roll.
   - Top with sautéed onions and peppers.
   - Spoon warm marinara sauce over the sausages.
   - Sprinkle with shredded cheese if using.
5. **Serve:**
   - Enjoy your Italian Sausage Sandwich hot!

This sandwich is hearty and full of savory flavors, perfect for a satisfying meal.

Turkey and Cranberry Sandwich

Ingredients:

- 2 slices of bread (whole grain, sourdough, or your choice)
- 4-6 slices of cooked turkey breast
- 2-3 tablespoons cranberry sauce (homemade or store-bought)
- 1-2 tablespoons mayonnaise (optional)
- 1-2 tablespoons mustard (optional)
- 1-2 lettuce leaves (optional)
- 1-2 slices of Swiss or cheddar cheese (optional)

Instructions:

1. **Prepare the Bread:**
   - Toast the bread slices if desired.
2. **Assemble the Sandwich:**
   - Spread mayonnaise and/or mustard on one side of each slice of bread if using.
   - Layer the turkey slices on one slice of bread.
   - Spoon cranberry sauce over the turkey.
   - Add cheese slices if desired.
   - Top with lettuce leaves if using.
   - Place the other slice of bread on top to complete the sandwich.
3. **Serve:**
   - Cut the sandwich in half if desired and enjoy!

This Turkey and Cranberry Sandwich is a delightful combination of savory turkey and sweet cranberry sauce, perfect for a festive lunch or a comforting meal.

Chicken Salad Sandwich

Ingredients:

- 2 cups cooked chicken breast, diced (can be shredded or cubed)
- 1/2 cup mayonnaise
- 1 tablespoon Dijon mustard
- 1/4 cup celery, finely chopped
- 1/4 cup red onion, finely chopped
- 1/4 cup sliced almonds or walnuts (optional)
- 1 tablespoon fresh parsley or dill, chopped (optional)
- Salt and pepper (to taste)
- 4 slices of bread (whole grain, white, or your choice)
- Lettuce leaves (optional)
- Tomato slices (optional)

Instructions:

1. **Prepare the Chicken Salad:**
    - In a large bowl, combine the diced chicken, mayonnaise, and Dijon mustard.
    - Add the chopped celery, red onion, and nuts if using.
    - Mix until well combined.
    - Season with salt and pepper to taste.
    - Stir in fresh parsley or dill if using.
2. **Prepare the Bread:**
    - Toast the bread slices if desired.
3. **Assemble the Sandwich:**
    - Spread a generous amount of chicken salad on one slice of bread.
    - Add lettuce leaves and tomato slices if desired.
    - Top with the other slice of bread.
4. **Serve:**
    - Slice the sandwich in half if desired and enjoy!

This Chicken Salad Sandwich is creamy and flavorful, making it a great choice for a satisfying lunch or a light dinner.

Eggplant Parmesan Sandwich

Ingredients:

- 1 large eggplant, sliced into 1/2-inch rounds
- 1 cup all-purpose flour
- 2 large eggs, beaten
- 1 cup breadcrumbs (plain or Italian seasoned)
- 1 cup marinara sauce
- 1 cup shredded mozzarella cheese
- 1/4 cup grated Parmesan cheese
- 4 slices of Italian or ciabatta bread
- Olive oil (for frying)
- Fresh basil leaves (optional, for garnish)
- Salt and pepper (to taste)

Instructions:

1. **Prepare the Eggplant:**
   - Preheat the oven to 400°F (200°C).
   - Season the eggplant slices with salt and let them sit for 15 minutes. Pat dry with paper towels.
2. **Bread the Eggplant:**
   - Set up a breading station: one bowl with flour, one with beaten eggs, and one with breadcrumbs.
   - Dredge each eggplant slice in flour, dip in the beaten eggs, then coat with breadcrumbs.
3. **Fry the Eggplant:**
   - Heat olive oil in a skillet over medium heat.
   - Fry the eggplant slices in batches until golden brown and crispy, about 3-4 minutes per side. Drain on paper towels.
4. **Assemble the Sandwich:**
   - Spread marinara sauce on one side of each bread slice.
   - Layer the fried eggplant slices on the sauce-covered side of two bread slices.
   - Top with mozzarella and Parmesan cheese.
   - Place the remaining bread slices on top, sauce side down.
5. **Toast the Sandwich:**
   - Heat a skillet over medium heat and add a little olive oil.
   - Cook the sandwiches until the bread is golden brown and the cheese is melted, about 3-4 minutes per side.
6. **Serve:**
   - Garnish with fresh basil if desired.
   - Slice the sandwiches in half and enjoy!

This Eggplant Parmesan Sandwich is a delicious vegetarian option with layers of crispy eggplant, melted cheese, and flavorful marinara.

PBLT (Pancetta, Bacon, Lettuce, Tomato)

Ingredients:

- 2 slices of bread (your choice, toasted if desired)
- 2 slices pancetta
- 2-3 slices bacon
- 1-2 leaves of lettuce
- 2 slices tomato
- 1 tablespoon mayonnaise (optional)
- 1 teaspoon Dijon mustard (optional)
- Salt and pepper (to taste)
- Olive oil (for frying)

Instructions:

1. **Cook the Pancetta and Bacon:**
   - Heat a skillet over medium heat and add a little olive oil.
   - Fry the pancetta until crispy, about 2-3 minutes per side. Remove and drain on paper towels.
   - In the same skillet, cook the bacon until crispy, about 4-5 minutes per side. Drain on paper towels.
2. **Prepare the Bread:**
   - Spread mayonnaise and/or Dijon mustard on one side of each bread slice if using.
3. **Assemble the Sandwich:**
   - Layer the pancetta and bacon on one slice of bread.
   - Add the lettuce leaves and tomato slices on top.
   - Season with salt and pepper to taste.
   - Place the other slice of bread on top.
4. **Serve:**
   - Slice the sandwich in half if desired and enjoy!

This PBLT sandwich is a crispy and delicious twist on the classic BLT, featuring rich pancetta and bacon.

Mushroom and Swiss Burger

Ingredients:

- 1 lb ground beef (80/20 for best flavor)
- 4 slices Swiss cheese
- 1 cup mushrooms, sliced
- 1 tablespoon olive oil
- 1 tablespoon butter
- 4 hamburger buns
- Lettuce leaves (optional)
- Tomato slices (optional)
- Salt and pepper (to taste)
- 1 tablespoon Worcestershire sauce (optional, for added flavor)

Instructions:

1. **Cook the Mushrooms:**
    - Heat olive oil and butter in a skillet over medium heat.
    - Add sliced mushrooms and cook until they are golden brown and tender, about 5-7 minutes. Season with salt and pepper.
2. **Prepare the Burgers:**
    - Divide the ground beef into 4 equal portions and shape into patties.
    - Season both sides with salt and pepper. If using Worcestershire sauce, mix it into the beef before forming patties.
3. **Cook the Burgers:**
    - Preheat a grill or skillet over medium-high heat.
    - Cook the burgers for about 4-5 minutes per side, or until they reach your desired level of doneness. Place a slice of Swiss cheese on each burger during the last minute of cooking to melt.
4. **Assemble the Burgers:**
    - Toast the hamburger buns if desired.
    - Place each burger patty with melted cheese on the bottom half of a bun.
    - Top with sautéed mushrooms.
    - Add lettuce and tomato slices if using.
    - Place the top half of the bun on the sandwich.
5. **Serve:**
    - Slice in half if desired and enjoy!

This Mushroom and Swiss Burger combines savory mushrooms with melted Swiss cheese for a deliciously satisfying meal.

Cheeseburger

Ingredients:

- 1 lb ground beef (80/20 for best flavor)
- 4 slices cheddar cheese (or your favorite cheese)
- 4 hamburger buns
- 1 tablespoon olive oil (for cooking)
- Salt and pepper (to taste)
- Optional toppings: lettuce, tomato, pickles, onions
- Optional condiments: ketchup, mustard, mayonnaise

Instructions:

1. **Prepare the Patties:**
   - Divide the ground beef into 4 equal portions and shape them into patties.
   - Season both sides of each patty with salt and pepper.
2. **Cook the Burgers:**
   - Heat olive oil in a skillet or on a grill over medium-high heat.
   - Cook the patties for about 4-5 minutes per side, or until they reach your desired doneness. During the last minute of cooking, place a slice of cheese on each patty to melt.
3. **Prepare the Buns:**
   - Toast the hamburger buns on the grill or in a toaster if desired.
4. **Assemble the Cheeseburgers:**
   - Spread condiments on the bottom half of each bun.
   - Place the cooked burger patty with melted cheese on top.
   - Add any optional toppings like lettuce, tomato, pickles, or onions.
   - Top with the other half of the bun.
5. **Serve:**
   - Serve hot and enjoy!

This classic Cheeseburger is juicy, cheesy, and customizable with your favorite toppings and condiments.

Pita Pocket with Falafel

Ingredients:

For the Falafel:

- 1 can (15 oz) chickpeas, drained and rinsed
- 1 small onion, roughly chopped
- 2 cloves garlic
- 1/2 cup fresh parsley, chopped
- 1/2 cup fresh cilantro, chopped
- 1 teaspoon ground cumin
- 1 teaspoon ground coriander
- 1/2 teaspoon baking powder
- 1/4 cup all-purpose flour
- Salt and pepper (to taste)
- Vegetable oil (for frying)

For the Pita Pocket:

- 4 pita bread pockets
- 1 cup shredded lettuce
- 1 cup cherry tomatoes, halved
- 1/2 cucumber, sliced
- 1/4 red onion, thinly sliced

For the Tahini Sauce (optional):

- 1/4 cup tahini
- 2 tablespoons lemon juice
- 1 clove garlic, minced
- 2-3 tablespoons water (to thin)
- Salt (to taste)

Instructions:

Prepare the Falafel:

1. **Blend the Ingredients:**
   - In a food processor, combine chickpeas, onion, garlic, parsley, cilantro, cumin, coriander, baking powder, and flour. Blend until a coarse, crumbly mixture forms. Season with salt and pepper.
2. **Form the Falafel:**
   - Shape the mixture into small balls or patties, about 1.5 inches in diameter.

3. **Fry the Falafel:**
   - Heat vegetable oil in a deep skillet or pan over medium heat. Fry the falafel balls in batches until golden brown and crispy, about 3-4 minutes per side. Drain on paper towels.

Prepare the Pita Pocket:

4. **Warm the Pita:**
   - Lightly toast or warm the pita bread in a toaster or oven if desired.
5. **Assemble the Pocket:**
   - Gently open each pita pocket and fill with shredded lettuce, cherry tomatoes, cucumber slices, and red onion.
6. **Add the Falafel:**
   - Stuff the pita pockets with the hot falafel balls.

Make the Tahini Sauce (Optional):

7. **Mix the Sauce:**
   - In a small bowl, whisk together tahini, lemon juice, minced garlic, and enough water to reach your desired consistency. Season with salt to taste.
8. **Serve:**
   - Drizzle tahini sauce over the falafel or serve on the side.

Enjoy your flavorful Pita Pocket with Falafel! This dish is perfect for a quick lunch or a satisfying dinner, packed with fresh ingredients and delicious flavors.

Lamb Gyro

Ingredients:

For the Lamb:

- 1 lb ground lamb
- 2 cloves garlic, minced
- 1 tablespoon ground cumin
- 1 tablespoon ground coriander
- 1 teaspoon dried oregano
- 1/2 teaspoon paprika
- 1/2 teaspoon ground cinnamon
- 1/2 teaspoon ground black pepper
- 1/2 teaspoon salt
- 1/4 cup fresh parsley, chopped

For the Tzatziki Sauce:

- 1 cup Greek yogurt
- 1/2 cucumber, grated and excess moisture squeezed out
- 2 cloves garlic, minced
- 1 tablespoon lemon juice
- 1 tablespoon fresh dill, chopped (or 1 teaspoon dried dill)
- Salt and pepper (to taste)

For Assembly:

- 4 pita bread or flatbreads
- 1 cup shredded lettuce
- 1 tomato, diced
- 1/4 red onion, thinly sliced
- Sliced olives (optional)

Instructions:

Prepare the Lamb:

1. **Mix Ingredients:**
    - In a large bowl, combine ground lamb, minced garlic, ground cumin, ground coriander, dried oregano, paprika, ground cinnamon, black pepper, salt, and chopped parsley. Mix until well combined.
2. **Form and Cook:**
    - Preheat your grill or a skillet over medium-high heat.

- Shape the lamb mixture into patties or form into a loaf for grilling.
- Grill the lamb patties or loaf for about 4-5 minutes per side, or until cooked through and browned. If using a skillet, you may need to cook in batches.

Prepare the Tzatziki Sauce:

3. **Mix Ingredients:**
   - In a bowl, combine Greek yogurt, grated cucumber, minced garlic, lemon juice, and dill. Stir until well mixed.
   - Season with salt and pepper to taste. Refrigerate until ready to use.

Assemble the Gyros:

4. **Warm the Pita:**
   - Warm the pita bread or flatbreads in a skillet, oven, or microwave.
5. **Assemble the Gyros:**
   - Spread some tzatziki sauce on the pita bread.
   - Layer with shredded lettuce, diced tomato, red onion slices, and olives if using.
   - Top with sliced lamb.
6. **Serve:**
   - Roll up the pita to enclose the filling and serve hot.

This Lamb Gyro is flavorful and satisfying, perfect for a casual meal or entertaining guests. Enjoy!

Thai Peanut Chicken Sandwich

Ingredients:

- 2 cups cooked chicken, shredded or sliced (grilled or rotisserie)
- 1/2 cup creamy peanut butter
- 2 tablespoons soy sauce
- 2 tablespoons honey
- 1 tablespoon rice vinegar or lime juice
- 1 teaspoon grated fresh ginger (optional)
- 1/2 cup shredded carrots
- 1/2 cup sliced cucumber
- 1/4 cup chopped fresh cilantro
- 4 slices of bread or rolls (brioche, ciabatta, or your choice)
- 1 tablespoon vegetable oil
- Salt and pepper (to taste)

Instructions:

1. **Prepare the Peanut Sauce:**
    - In a bowl, whisk together peanut butter, soy sauce, honey, rice vinegar (or lime juice), and grated ginger until smooth. Adjust seasoning with salt and pepper if needed.
2. **Mix the Chicken:**
    - Toss the shredded or sliced chicken with the peanut sauce until well coated.
3. **Prepare the Vegetables:**
    - Slice the cucumber and chop the cilantro.
4. **Toast the Bread:**
    - Heat a skillet over medium heat and lightly toast the bread slices or rolls in vegetable oil until golden brown and crispy.
5. **Assemble the Sandwich:**
    - Spread some of the peanut sauce on one side of each toasted bread slice.
    - Layer with the peanut sauce-coated chicken.
    - Top with shredded carrots, cucumber slices, and chopped cilantro.
    - Place the other slice of bread on top.
6. **Serve:**
    - Cut the sandwich in half if desired and enjoy!

This Thai Peanut Chicken Sandwich combines the rich flavors of peanut sauce with fresh vegetables for a deliciously unique twist on a classic chicken sandwich.

Breakfast Burrito Wrap

Ingredients:

- 4 large flour tortillas
- 4 large eggs
- 1/4 cup milk
- 1 cup cooked and crumbled breakfast sausage or bacon
- 1 cup shredded cheddar cheese
- 1/2 cup cooked and diced potatoes (optional)
- 1/2 cup salsa or pico de gallo
- 1 tablespoon olive oil
- Salt and pepper (to taste)
- Optional: chopped green onions, avocado slices, sour cream

Instructions:

1. **Prepare the Filling:**
   - In a bowl, whisk together eggs, milk, salt, and pepper.
   - Heat olive oil in a skillet over medium heat.
   - Pour in the egg mixture and cook, stirring occasionally, until scrambled and fully cooked. Remove from heat.
2. **Assemble the Burritos:**
   - Warm the tortillas in a dry skillet or microwave to make them more pliable.
   - Lay out each tortilla and spread a layer of cooked potatoes (if using) in the center.
   - Top with scrambled eggs, crumbled sausage or bacon, and shredded cheddar cheese.
   - Spoon some salsa or pico de gallo over the filling.
   - Add any optional toppings like chopped green onions or avocado slices.
3. **Wrap the Burritos:**
   - Fold the sides of the tortilla over the filling, then roll from the bottom up to form a wrap.
   - For a crispier burrito, heat a skillet over medium heat and cook each burrito seam-side down until golden and crispy, about 2-3 minutes per side.
4. **Serve:**
   - Serve hot with extra salsa or sour cream if desired.

This Breakfast Burrito Wrap is a delicious and filling way to start your day, packed with protein and flavor!

Lobster Roll

Ingredients:

- 1 lb cooked lobster meat, chopped into bite-sized pieces (about 2 cups)
- 1/4 cup mayonnaise
- 1 tablespoon lemon juice
- 1 tablespoon chopped fresh chives or parsley
- 1 teaspoon Dijon mustard
- 1/2 teaspoon Old Bay seasoning (optional)
- Salt and pepper (to taste)
- 4 hot dog buns or split-top rolls
- 2 tablespoons butter (for toasting buns)
- Lemon wedges (for serving, optional)

Instructions:

1. **Prepare the Lobster Salad:**
   - In a bowl, combine the chopped lobster meat with mayonnaise, lemon juice, chopped chives (or parsley), Dijon mustard, and Old Bay seasoning (if using).
   - Gently mix until the lobster is well coated. Season with salt and pepper to taste.
2. **Toast the Buns:**
   - Heat a skillet over medium heat.
   - Spread butter on the outside of each bun.
   - Place the buns in the skillet and toast until golden brown on each side, about 2-3 minutes.
3. **Assemble the Lobster Rolls:**
   - Spoon the lobster salad generously into each toasted bun.
4. **Serve:**
   - Serve immediately with lemon wedges on the side if desired.

This Lobster Roll is a delicious treat, combining tender lobster meat with a light, creamy dressing and served in a buttery, toasted bun. Perfect for a special occasion or a summery meal!

Corned Beef on Rye

Ingredients:

- 4 slices rye bread
- 8 oz sliced corned beef
- 2 tablespoons yellow mustard (or to taste)
- 1/2 cup sauerkraut, drained
- 4 slices Swiss cheese
- 1 tablespoon butter (for grilling)

Instructions:

1. **Prepare the Sandwich:**
   - Spread mustard on one side of each slice of rye bread.
2. **Assemble the Sandwich:**
   - On two slices of bread, layer corned beef, Swiss cheese, and sauerkraut.
   - Top with the remaining slices of bread, mustard side down.
3. **Grill the Sandwich:**
   - Heat butter in a skillet over medium heat.
   - Place the sandwiches in the skillet and cook until golden brown and the cheese is melted, about 3-4 minutes per side.
4. **Serve:**
   - Slice the sandwiches in half if desired and enjoy!

This Corned Beef on Rye is a classic deli favorite, combining savory corned beef with melted cheese and tangy sauerkraut.

Falafel Sandwich

Ingredients:

For the Falafel:

- 1 can (15 oz) chickpeas, drained and rinsed
- 1 small onion, roughly chopped
- 2 cloves garlic
- 1/2 cup fresh parsley, chopped
- 1/2 cup fresh cilantro, chopped
- 1 teaspoon ground cumin
- 1 teaspoon ground coriander
- 1/2 teaspoon baking powder
- 1/4 cup all-purpose flour
- Salt and pepper (to taste)
- Vegetable oil (for frying)

For the Sandwich:

- 4 pita bread pockets
- 1 cup shredded lettuce
- 1/2 cup diced tomatoes
- 1/2 cucumber, sliced
- 1/4 red onion, thinly sliced
- 1/2 cup hummus or tahini sauce (optional)

Instructions:

Prepare the Falafel:

1. **Blend the Ingredients:**
   - In a food processor, combine chickpeas, onion, garlic, parsley, cilantro, cumin, coriander, baking powder, and flour. Blend until a coarse, crumbly mixture forms. Season with salt and pepper.
2. **Form and Fry the Falafel:**
   - Shape the mixture into small balls or patties.
   - Heat vegetable oil in a skillet over medium heat.
   - Fry the falafel balls in batches until golden brown and crispy, about 3-4 minutes per side. Drain on paper towels.

Assemble the Sandwich:

3. **Warm the Pita:**

        - Lightly toast or warm the pita bread if desired.
4. **Fill the Pita:**
        - Gently open each pita pocket and fill with shredded lettuce, diced tomatoes, cucumber slices, and red onion.
        - Add the hot falafel balls on top.
        - Spread hummus or tahini sauce inside the pita if using.
5. **Serve:**
        - Serve the sandwiches hot, and enjoy!

This Falafel Sandwich is packed with flavor and fresh veggies, making it a great vegetarian option for a quick and satisfying meal.

Grilled Veggie Sandwich

Ingredients:

- 1 large eggplant, sliced into 1/4-inch rounds
- 1 large zucchini, sliced into 1/4-inch rounds
- 1 red bell pepper, sliced into strips
- 1 yellow bell pepper, sliced into strips
- 1 red onion, sliced into rings
- 2-3 tablespoons olive oil
- Salt and pepper (to taste)
- 4 slices of your favorite bread (ciabatta, sourdough, or whole grain work well)
- 1/2 cup hummus or pesto (optional, for spreading)
- 4-6 slices of provolone or mozzarella cheese (optional)
- Fresh basil or spinach (optional, for added freshness)

Instructions:

1. **Prepare the Vegetables:**
    - Preheat your grill or a grill pan over medium-high heat.
    - Toss the eggplant, zucchini, bell peppers, and red onion with olive oil, salt, and pepper.
2. **Grill the Vegetables:**
    - Grill the vegetables in batches, turning occasionally, until tender and slightly charred, about 4-5 minutes per side. Remove from heat and set aside.
3. **Prepare the Bread:**
    - If using, spread hummus or pesto on one side of each slice of bread.
4. **Assemble the Sandwich:**
    - Layer the grilled vegetables on half of the bread slices.
    - If using cheese, place a slice or two on top of the vegetables.
    - Add fresh basil or spinach if desired.
    - Top with the remaining slices of bread.
5. **Grill the Sandwich:**
    - Heat a skillet over medium heat. Add a little olive oil or butter if desired.
    - Place the sandwiches in the skillet and cook until the bread is golden brown and the cheese is melted, about 3-4 minutes per side.
6. **Serve:**
    - Slice in half if desired and serve hot.

This Grilled Veggie Sandwich is full of savory grilled vegetables and can be customized with your favorite spreads and cheese. It's perfect for a satisfying lunch or light dinner!

Hot Ham and Cheese

Ingredients:

- 4 slices of bread (white, whole grain, or your choice)
- 4 slices of deli ham
- 4 slices of cheese (Swiss, cheddar, or your preference)
- 2 tablespoons butter (for grilling)
- 1 tablespoon Dijon mustard (optional)
- 1 tablespoon mayonnaise (optional)

Instructions:

1. **Prepare the Bread:**
    - If using, spread Dijon mustard and/or mayonnaise on one side of each slice of bread.
2. **Assemble the Sandwich:**
    - On two slices of bread, layer 2 slices of ham and 2 slices of cheese.
    - Top with the remaining slices of bread, mustard or mayo side down.
3. **Grill the Sandwich:**
    - Heat a skillet over medium heat.
    - Spread butter on the outside of each slice of bread.
    - Place the sandwiches in the skillet and cook until golden brown and the cheese is melted, about 3-4 minutes per side. Press down gently with a spatula for an even grill.
4. **Serve:**
    - Slice the sandwiches in half if desired and enjoy!

This Hot Ham and Cheese Sandwich is a timeless classic, perfect for a quick and comforting meal.

Spicy Italian Sub

Ingredients:

- 1 Italian sub roll or hoagie roll
- 4 slices of salami
- 4 slices of pepperoni
- 4 slices of provolone or mozzarella cheese
- 4 slices of capicola (or another Italian cured meat)
- 1/2 cup sliced pickled hot peppers or banana peppers
- 1/4 cup sliced black olives
- 1/2 cup shredded lettuce
- 1/2 tomato, thinly sliced
- 1/4 red onion, thinly sliced
- 2 tablespoons mayonnaise (optional)
- 1 tablespoon Dijon mustard (optional)
- 1 tablespoon olive oil
- 1 tablespoon red wine vinegar
- Salt and pepper (to taste)

Instructions:

1. **Prepare the Roll:**
   - Cut the Italian sub roll lengthwise, but don't cut all the way through; leave a hinge.
2. **Assemble the Sandwich:**
   - If using, spread mayonnaise and Dijon mustard on the inside of the roll.
   - Layer the salami, pepperoni, provolone or mozzarella cheese, and capicola on the bottom half of the roll.
   - Add pickled hot peppers, black olives, shredded lettuce, tomato slices, and red onion.
3. **Prepare the Dressing:**
   - In a small bowl, whisk together olive oil, red wine vinegar, salt, and pepper.
   - Drizzle the dressing over the sandwich fillings.
4. **Serve:**
   - Close the sandwich and cut in half if desired. Enjoy immediately, or wrap in foil for a tasty on-the-go meal.

This Spicy Italian Sub is packed with zesty Italian meats, spicy peppers, and a tangy dressing, making it a flavorful and satisfying sandwich.

Chicken and Waffles Sandwich

Ingredients:

For the Chicken:

- 2 boneless, skinless chicken breasts
- 1 cup buttermilk
- 1 cup all-purpose flour
- 1 teaspoon paprika
- 1/2 teaspoon garlic powder
- 1/2 teaspoon onion powder
- 1/2 teaspoon cayenne pepper (optional, for heat)
- Salt and pepper (to taste)
- Vegetable oil (for frying)

For the Waffles:

- 4 frozen or homemade waffles (your choice)
- 1 tablespoon butter (for grilling waffles, optional)

For Assembly:

- Maple syrup (for drizzling)
- Optional: hot sauce, pickles, or coleslaw

Instructions:

Prepare the Chicken:

1. **Marinate:**
    - Place chicken breasts in a bowl with buttermilk. Cover and refrigerate for at least 1 hour or overnight for best results.
2. **Coat and Fry:**
    - In a bowl, mix flour, paprika, garlic powder, onion powder, cayenne pepper, salt, and pepper.
    - Remove chicken from buttermilk, allowing excess to drip off, then coat in the flour mixture.
    - Heat vegetable oil in a skillet over medium-high heat.
    - Fry chicken for about 5-7 minutes per side, or until golden brown and cooked through. Drain on paper towels.

Prepare the Waffles:

3. **Toast Waffles:**

- If using frozen waffles, toast according to package instructions.
- For a crispier texture, lightly butter the waffles and grill in a skillet over medium heat until golden brown.

Assemble the Sandwich:

4. **Build the Sandwich:**
     - Place one waffle on a plate.
     - Top with the fried chicken breast.
     - Drizzle with maple syrup and add any optional ingredients like hot sauce, pickles, or coleslaw if desired.
     - Top with another waffle to complete the sandwich.
5. **Serve:**
     - Serve hot and enjoy!

This Chicken and Waffles Sandwich combines sweet and savory elements for a unique and delicious meal.

Crispy Fish Sandwich

Ingredients:

For the Fish:

- 4 fish fillets (such as cod, haddock, or tilapia), about 4-6 oz each
- 1 cup all-purpose flour
- 1 cup cornmeal
- 1 teaspoon paprika
- 1 teaspoon garlic powder
- 1/2 teaspoon onion powder
- 1/2 teaspoon cayenne pepper (optional, for heat)
- 1 teaspoon salt
- 1/2 teaspoon black pepper
- 1 cup buttermilk (or milk)
- Vegetable oil (for frying)

For the Sandwich:

- 4 sandwich rolls or hamburger buns
- 1 cup shredded lettuce
- 1 tomato, sliced
- 1/4 red onion, thinly sliced
- Pickles (optional)
- 1/4 cup tartar sauce or mayonnaise (optional)

Instructions:

Prepare the Fish:

1. **Preheat the Oil:**
   - Heat vegetable oil in a large skillet or deep fryer over medium-high heat to 350°F (175°C).
2. **Prepare the Breading:**
   - In one bowl, place the flour.
   - In another bowl, mix the cornmeal, paprika, garlic powder, onion powder, cayenne pepper (if using), salt, and pepper.
   - In a third bowl, pour the buttermilk (or milk).
3. **Coat the Fish:**
   - Dip each fish fillet into the flour, coating it evenly.
   - Dip the floured fillet into the buttermilk, letting excess drip off.
   - Coat the fillet in the cornmeal mixture, pressing gently to adhere.
4. **Fry the Fish:**

- Fry the fish fillets in batches, being careful not to overcrowd the pan. Cook until golden brown and crispy, about 4-5 minutes per side.
- Drain on paper towels.

Prepare the Sandwich:

5. **Toast the Buns:**
   - Lightly toast the sandwich rolls or buns in a skillet or oven if desired.
6. **Assemble the Sandwich:**
   - Spread tartar sauce or mayonnaise on the bottom half of each roll.
   - Place a crispy fish fillet on each roll.
   - Top with shredded lettuce, tomato slices, red onion, and pickles if using.
   - Cover with the top half of the roll.
7. **Serve:**
   - Serve the sandwiches hot and enjoy!

This Crispy Fish Sandwich is packed with flavor and crunch, making it a satisfying and classic choice for a quick meal.

Tandoori Chicken Sandwich

Ingredients:

For the Tandoori Chicken:

- 2 boneless, skinless chicken breasts
- 1 cup plain yogurt
- 2 tablespoons tandoori masala (store-bought or homemade)
- 1 tablespoon lemon juice
- 1 tablespoon minced garlic
- 1 tablespoon minced ginger
- 1 teaspoon ground cumin
- 1 teaspoon ground coriander
- 1/2 teaspoon turmeric
- Salt and pepper (to taste)

For the Sandwich:

- 4 sandwich rolls or ciabatta rolls
- 1/2 cup shredded lettuce
- 1/2 red onion, thinly sliced
- 1 tomato, sliced
- 1/4 cup mint chutney or yogurt sauce (optional, for spreading)

Instructions:

Prepare the Tandoori Chicken:

1. **Marinate the Chicken:**
   - In a bowl, combine yogurt, tandoori masala, lemon juice, garlic, ginger, cumin, coriander, turmeric, salt, and pepper.
   - Add the chicken breasts, ensuring they are fully coated. Cover and refrigerate for at least 1 hour, preferably overnight.
2. **Cook the Chicken:**
   - Preheat your grill or oven to medium-high heat.
   - Grill or bake the chicken until cooked through and slightly charred, about 5-7 minutes per side on the grill, or 20-25 minutes in the oven at 375°F (190°C). Slice into strips or pieces.

Prepare the Sandwich:

3. **Toast the Rolls:**
   - Lightly toast the sandwich rolls in a toaster or under the broiler.

4. **Assemble the Sandwich:**
    - If using, spread mint chutney or yogurt sauce on the inside of each roll.
    - Layer with shredded lettuce, sliced tandoori chicken, red onion, and tomato slices.
5. **Serve:**
    - Close the sandwich and serve hot.

This Tandoori Chicken Sandwich offers a delightful blend of spicy, tangy flavors and is perfect for a satisfying meal with a touch of Indian flair.

Pulled Beef Brisket Sandwich

Ingredients:

For the Brisket:

- 3-4 lbs beef brisket
- 1 tablespoon olive oil
- 2 tablespoons smoked paprika
- 1 tablespoon garlic powder
- 1 tablespoon onion powder
- 1 tablespoon brown sugar
- 1 tablespoon ground cumin
- 1 teaspoon black pepper
- 1 teaspoon salt
- 1 cup beef broth or water
- 1/2 cup BBQ sauce (optional, for added flavor)

For the Sandwich:

- 4 sandwich rolls or hamburger buns
- 1 cup coleslaw (store-bought or homemade)
- 1/4 cup BBQ sauce (optional, for serving)
- Pickles (optional)

Instructions:

Prepare the Brisket:

1. **Season the Brisket:**
   - In a small bowl, mix smoked paprika, garlic powder, onion powder, brown sugar, cumin, black pepper, and salt.
   - Rub the spice mixture evenly over the brisket.
2. **Cook the Brisket:**
   - Heat olive oil in a large skillet or Dutch oven over medium-high heat. Sear the brisket on all sides until browned, about 4-5 minutes per side.
   - Transfer the brisket to a slow cooker. Add beef broth or water.
   - Cover and cook on low for 8-10 hours, or until the brisket is tender and easily shreds with a fork.
3. **Shred the Brisket:**
   - Remove the brisket from the slow cooker and shred the meat with two forks. Return the shredded meat to the slow cooker and mix with the cooking juices. Stir in BBQ sauce if desired.

Prepare the Sandwich:

4. **Toast the Rolls:**
    - Lightly toast the sandwich rolls in a toaster or under the broiler if desired.
5. **Assemble the Sandwich:**
    - Pile the pulled brisket onto the bottom half of each roll.
    - Top with coleslaw and additional BBQ sauce if desired.
    - Add pickles if using, then cover with the top half of the roll.
6. **Serve:**
    - Serve the sandwiches hot and enjoy!

This Pulled Beef Brisket Sandwich is packed with rich, smoky flavors and topped with crunchy coleslaw, making it a hearty and satisfying meal.

Pork Schnitzel Sandwich

Ingredients:

For the Schnitzel:

- 4 pork loin cutlets (about 1/2 inch thick)
- 1 cup all-purpose flour
- 2 large eggs
- 1 cup breadcrumbs (preferably panko for extra crispiness)
- 1/2 cup grated Parmesan cheese (optional)
- Salt and pepper (to taste)
- Vegetable oil (for frying)

For the Sandwich:

- 4 sandwich rolls or ciabatta rolls
- 1/2 cup Dijon mustard or mayonnaise (optional)
- 4 slices Swiss cheese (or your preferred cheese)
- 1 cup shredded lettuce
- 1 tomato, sliced
- 1/4 red onion, thinly sliced
- Pickles (optional)

Instructions:

Prepare the Schnitzel:

1. **Pound the Pork:**
    - Place each pork cutlet between two sheets of plastic wrap or parchment paper. Pound with a meat mallet or rolling pin until about 1/4 inch thick.
2. **Bread the Schnitzel:**
    - Set up a breading station: place flour in one shallow dish, beat eggs in another, and mix breadcrumbs with Parmesan cheese (if using) in a third dish.
    - Season the pork cutlets with salt and pepper.
    - Dredge each cutlet in flour, shaking off excess, then dip in beaten eggs, and coat evenly with breadcrumbs.
3. **Fry the Schnitzel:**
    - Heat vegetable oil in a large skillet over medium-high heat.
    - Fry the breaded pork cutlets until golden brown and cooked through, about 3-4 minutes per side. Drain on paper towels.

Prepare the Sandwich:

4. **Toast the Rolls:**
    - Lightly toast the sandwich rolls in a toaster or under the broiler if desired.
5. **Assemble the Sandwich:**
    - Spread Dijon mustard or mayonnaise on the inside of each roll if desired.
    - Place a hot schnitzel on the bottom half of each roll.
    - Top with a slice of Swiss cheese, shredded lettuce, tomato slices, red onion, and pickles if using.
    - Cover with the top half of the roll.
6. **Serve:**
    - Serve the sandwiches hot and enjoy!

This Pork Schnitzel Sandwich is crispy and flavorful, combining tender pork with fresh veggies and melted cheese for a satisfying meal.

Pork Belly Banh Mi

Ingredients:

For the Pork Belly:

- 1 lb pork belly, skinless
- 2 tablespoons soy sauce
- 1 tablespoon fish sauce
- 2 tablespoons brown sugar
- 1 tablespoon hoisin sauce
- 1 tablespoon rice vinegar
- 3 cloves garlic, minced
- 1 tablespoon grated ginger
- 1/2 teaspoon five-spice powder (optional)

For the Pickled Vegetables:

- 1 cup julienned carrots
- 1 cup julienned daikon radish
- 1/2 cup rice vinegar
- 1/2 cup water
- 1/4 cup sugar
- 1 teaspoon salt

For the Sandwich:

- 4 French baguettes or Vietnamese baguettes
- 1/2 cup mayonnaise
- 1-2 tablespoons sriracha or chili sauce (optional, for heat)
- 1 cucumber, sliced thinly
- Fresh cilantro leaves
- Sliced jalapeños (optional, for added heat)

Instructions:

Prepare the Pork Belly:

1. **Marinate the Pork:**
    - Preheat your oven to 325°F (165°C).
    - In a bowl, combine soy sauce, fish sauce, brown sugar, hoisin sauce, rice vinegar, garlic, ginger, and five-spice powder (if using).
    - Place the pork belly in a baking dish and pour the marinade over it. Cover and refrigerate for at least 1 hour or overnight.

2. **Roast the Pork:**
   - Remove the pork belly from the marinade and place it in a roasting pan, skin side up.
   - Roast in the preheated oven for about 1.5 to 2 hours, or until the pork is tender and the skin is crispy. Baste occasionally with the marinade.
   - Let the pork rest for 10 minutes before slicing into thin strips.

Prepare the Pickled Vegetables:

3. **Pickle the Vegetables:**
   - In a bowl, whisk together rice vinegar, water, sugar, and salt until dissolved.
   - Add the julienned carrots and daikon radish, and let them pickle for at least 30 minutes.

Prepare the Sandwich:

4. **Prepare the Baguettes:**
   - Lightly toast the baguettes if desired.
5. **Assemble the Sandwich:**
   - Mix mayonnaise with sriracha or chili sauce if using.
   - Spread the spicy mayo on the inside of each baguette.
   - Layer in the sliced pork belly, pickled vegetables, cucumber slices, fresh cilantro, and sliced jalapeños if using.
6. **Serve:**
   - Serve the sandwiches immediately and enjoy!

This Pork Belly Banh Mi is a delightful fusion of flavors with crispy pork belly, tangy pickled vegetables, and fresh herbs, all in a crunchy baguette.

Roasted Red Pepper and Goat Cheese Sandwich

Ingredients:

- 4 slices of bread (sourdough, ciabatta, or your choice)
- 1 jar (12 oz) roasted red peppers, drained and sliced
- 4 oz goat cheese, softened
- 1 tablespoon olive oil
- 1 clove garlic, minced
- 1 cup fresh basil leaves (or spinach if preferred)
- Salt and pepper (to taste)

Instructions:

1. **Prepare the Spread:**
   - In a small bowl, mix softened goat cheese with minced garlic. Season with salt and pepper.
2. **Assemble the Sandwich:**
   - Spread the goat cheese mixture evenly on two slices of bread.
   - Layer with roasted red pepper slices and fresh basil leaves.
3. **Toast the Sandwich:**
   - Heat olive oil in a skillet over medium heat.
   - Place the sandwiches in the skillet and cook until golden brown and the cheese is slightly melted, about 3-4 minutes per side.
4. **Serve:**
   - Slice in half if desired and serve hot.

This Roasted Red Pepper and Goat Cheese Sandwich combines creamy goat cheese with sweet, smoky peppers and fresh basil for a deliciously satisfying meal.

Cheddar and Apple Sandwich

Ingredients:

- 2 slices of bread (sourdough, whole grain, or your choice)
- 4 oz sharp cheddar cheese, sliced
- 1 apple (such as Honeycrisp or Granny Smith), cored and thinly sliced
- 1 tablespoon Dijon mustard (optional)
- 1 tablespoon honey or apple butter (optional)
- 1 tablespoon butter (for grilling)

Instructions:

1. **Prepare the Spread:**
   - Spread Dijon mustard and/or honey or apple butter on one side of each slice of bread if using.
2. **Assemble the Sandwich:**
   - Layer cheddar cheese and apple slices on one slice of bread.
   - Top with the second slice of bread.
3. **Grill the Sandwich:**
   - Heat butter in a skillet over medium heat.
   - Place the sandwich in the skillet and cook until golden brown and the cheese is melted, about 3-4 minutes per side.
4. **Serve:**
   - Slice in half if desired and enjoy!

This Cheddar and Apple Sandwich offers a delightful combination of sharp cheddar and sweet, crisp apples, making it a refreshing and satisfying choice.

Black Bean and Avocado Wrap

Ingredients:

- 1 can (15 oz) black beans, drained and rinsed
- 1 ripe avocado, sliced
- 1 cup corn kernels (fresh, frozen, or canned)
- 1/2 red bell pepper, diced
- 1/4 red onion, finely chopped
- 1/2 cup cherry tomatoes, halved
- 1 cup shredded lettuce or baby spinach
- 1/4 cup fresh cilantro, chopped
- Juice of 1 lime
- 1/2 teaspoon ground cumin
- 1/2 teaspoon paprika
- Salt and pepper (to taste)
- 4 large flour or whole wheat tortillas
- Optional: sour cream or Greek yogurt, for serving

Instructions:

1. **Prepare the Bean Mixture:**
    - In a bowl, combine black beans, corn, red bell pepper, red onion, cherry tomatoes, and cilantro.
    - Add lime juice, ground cumin, paprika, salt, and pepper. Toss to combine.
2. **Prepare the Wrap:**
    - Lay out the tortillas on a flat surface.
    - Spread a layer of shredded lettuce or baby spinach on each tortilla.
    - Distribute the black bean mixture evenly over the lettuce.
    - Top with slices of avocado.
3. **Wrap It Up:**
    - Fold in the sides of the tortilla and then roll it up from the bottom, securing the filling inside.
4. **Serve:**
    - Slice in half if desired and serve with optional sour cream or Greek yogurt on the side.

This Black Bean and Avocado Wrap is packed with fresh flavors, healthy ingredients, and is perfect for a quick lunch or light dinner.

Buffalo Cauliflower Sandwich

Ingredients:

For the Buffalo Cauliflower:

- 1 large head of cauliflower, cut into florets
- 1 cup all-purpose flour
- 1 cup buttermilk (or milk with 1 tablespoon lemon juice)
- 1 teaspoon garlic powder
- 1 teaspoon onion powder
- 1/2 teaspoon smoked paprika
- Salt and pepper (to taste)
- 1 cup breadcrumbs (preferably panko)
- 1 cup buffalo sauce

For the Sandwich:

- 4 sandwich rolls or burger buns
- 1 cup shredded lettuce
- 1/2 cup sliced pickles
- 1/4 cup ranch or blue cheese dressing (optional, for serving)

Instructions:

Prepare the Cauliflower:

1. **Preheat Oven:**
   - Preheat your oven to 425°F (220°C). Line a baking sheet with parchment paper.
2. **Coat the Cauliflower:**
   - In a bowl, whisk together flour, garlic powder, onion powder, smoked paprika, salt, and pepper.
   - Dip cauliflower florets into the buttermilk, then coat with the flour mixture.
   - Dredge in breadcrumbs, pressing gently to adhere.
3. **Bake the Cauliflower:**
   - Arrange the coated cauliflower on the prepared baking sheet.
   - Bake for 25-30 minutes, or until crispy and golden brown, flipping halfway through.
4. **Toss in Buffalo Sauce:**
   - In a large bowl, toss the baked cauliflower with buffalo sauce until well coated.

Prepare the Sandwich:

5. **Toast the Rolls:**

- Lightly toast the sandwich rolls or buns if desired.
6. **Assemble the Sandwich:**
    - Spread ranch or blue cheese dressing on the bottom half of each roll if using.
    - Top with buffalo cauliflower, shredded lettuce, and pickles.
    - Cover with the top half of the roll.
7. **Serve:**
    - Serve the sandwiches hot and enjoy!

This Buffalo Cauliflower Sandwich offers a spicy, crispy twist on a classic sandwich, perfect for a hearty, plant-based meal.

www.ingramcontent.com/pod-product-compliance
Lightning Source LLC
LaVergne TN
LVHW081317060526
838201LV00055B/2325

9798330375745